FOUNDATION LEVEL 2

Collins

LITTLE LEARNERS

ART AND CRAFT

SERIES EDITOR: RANI T.

Student + Teacher			**Teacher-only**	
a animations	ia activities	g games	lp lesson plans	tn teacher's notes
ilt instructor-led tutorials	w worksheets	v videos	w worksheets	ak answer keys
	audio			

Preface

Collins Little Learners, comprising 20 books in all, provides graded, age-appropriate learning opportunities targeting holistic skill development for children in the age group of 3 years to 6 years. Spread across three levels, the series spans **English**, **Maths**, **General Awareness**, **Art and Craft** and **Hindi**. The series comes bundled with a **workbook** for English and a book of **rhymes and stories** for each level. The books use a combination of hands-on activities, frequent recapitulation and child-friendly artwork to facilitate learning.

The early years are the most significant years for growth, development and learning. During this period, children need adequate opportunities for stimulating experiences as these favourably affect various learning abilities. Learning experiences, when chosen and planned properly, fuel the innate curiosity of children, and stimulate their thought processes.

Learning and Development During the Early Years

The goal of learning during the early years is to enhance the all-round development of personality and to inculcate healthy attitudes, life skills and good values. Creative play, well thought-out games and developmentally appropriate activities help children develop the necessary skills to achieve these goals. The skills that children need to acquire can broadly be categorized as:

Motor: Motor skills pertain not only to gross motor activities like walking and jumping but also include fine motor activities like the ability to hold a pencil and write. The development of motor skills is facilitated through several graded activities.

Personal, Social and Emotional: Personal, social and emotional development, necessary for the overall personality development of children, is achieved using a combination of hands-on activities, role plays, and thought-provoking stories and rhymes.

Linguistic: The ability to listen, speak, read and write is critical to success in formal learning environments.

Mathematical: The development of mathematical ideas and concepts is important at this stage since children will continue to build on this learning for most of their years of schooling.

Knowledge and Understanding of the World: This is achieved through activities that enable children to explore their surroundings at home and in the school, and interact with the people that they see around them.

Health and Safety: The idea of health and safety is introduced through activities, stories and retelling of real-life experiences to encourage children to focus on health and well-being.

Creative: Creative skills are developed through a host of activities involving art, craft, painting, roleplays, etc.

Logical and Rational Thinking: Activities that involve simple puzzles, pattern-completion and visual discrimination help children develop logical and rational thinking skills.

The Collins Little Learners Teacher Support Materials

The series includes extensive teacher support in the form of:

Teacher's Resource Books: Comprises stories, activity banks, classroom management and assessment guidelines

Multimedia eBook: Consists of animations, audio, video, slide shows, and interactive exercises

Print-ready Worksheets: Additional worksheets for practice and reinforcement, present in the digital support

Digital Flashcards: Flashcards with embedded sounds and animations for letter formation and letter-sound association

Animations and Songs: Animated stories and rhymes set to tune

Interactive Games: Interactivities to reinforce concepts in a fun and engaging manner

A note on the activity banks (included in the Teacher's Manuals)

The activity banks comprise hands-on activities that will help children develop the requisite skills to attain age-appropriate learning goals. In keeping with Howard Gardener's theory of multiple intelligences, the activity banks include options and variations that enable teachers to provide a planned cycle of experiences and opportunities, which foster each type of intelligence, to every child in their classrooms. The activity banks equip teachers to use the strengths of children as a means of complementing their less developed areas by valuing and nurturing the inherent abilities of the children.

Contents

Walkthrough

A variety of tracing and colouring activities to further fine motor development in an enjoyable manner

Free-hand drawing and colouring pages to support creative development

Rolling, flattening and shaping modelling clay and cotton to support motor development

Tearing, pasting, cutting to improve hand-eye coordination and develop the ability to grip objects

Cross-curricular linkages in activities to help support overall learning development

Luminous Lamp

Make a lamp with the letter L. Decorate it as you like.

Material Required

Orange/yellow origami paper, child-safe scissors, black wool, decorative material and glue

Procedure

Draw the shape of the lampshade on the origami paper. Encourage children to cut the paper along the lines independently. Children should paste black wool next to the letter 'L'. Paste the paper in the space provided. Allow children to decorate the lampshade as they like.

Cute Caterpillar

Paste woollen threads in spirals to make the caterpillar.

Procedure

Help children cut wool into small pieces. Encourage children to paste the wool independently. Demonstrate how to paste the lengths of wool in a spiral manner.

Material Required

Woollen threads, child-safe scissors, googly eyes and glue

Underwater World

Colour the animals. Count and write the number of animals.

Procedure

Allow children to colour all the animals. They can use any colour they like. Make sure that they use a single colour for one kind of creature. They can then count and use sketch pens to write numbers of creatures in the aquarium.

Material Required

Crayons and sketch pens

Cluck-Cluck Chicks

Print your hands to make chicks.

Procedure

Demonstrate how to dip the hand in yellow paint and print on the paper. Children should be guided to place their thumbs just below the crowns of hens.

Material Required

Yellow poster colour and black sketch pen

Shape Rocket

Make a rocket with different shapes.

Procedure

Encourage children to cut out the required shapes of origami paper to make a rocket. To show the trail of smoke coming out of the rocket, children can paste cotton at the bottom edge of the rocket. To make clouds they can be asked to paste cotton again. They can decorate the rocket with decorative material as they like.

Material Required

Origami paper, cotton, decorative material, child-safe scissors and glue

My Fruit Basket

Complete the fruit basket. Colour the details of fruits.

Procedure

Explain that a different method is used to make each fruit. Cut and paste red origami paper to make the apple. Paste lengths of yellow wool to make the banana. Paste green beads to make the pear. Crush and paste small pieces of orange origami paper to make the orange. Thumbprint using purple/green poster colour to make the grapes. Use crayons to colour the pineapple. Use maroon sparkle to make the cherries.

Material Required

Beads, wool, red and orange origami paper, crayons, purple/green poster colour, maroon sparkle, child-safe scissors and glue

Colourful Canopy

Use colourful cotton balls to make the umbrella.

Procedure

Demonstrate how to paste cotton balls of the same colour in each section of the umbrella.

Material Required

Colourful cotton balls and glue

The Queen's Dress

Use okra to print the dress of the queen.

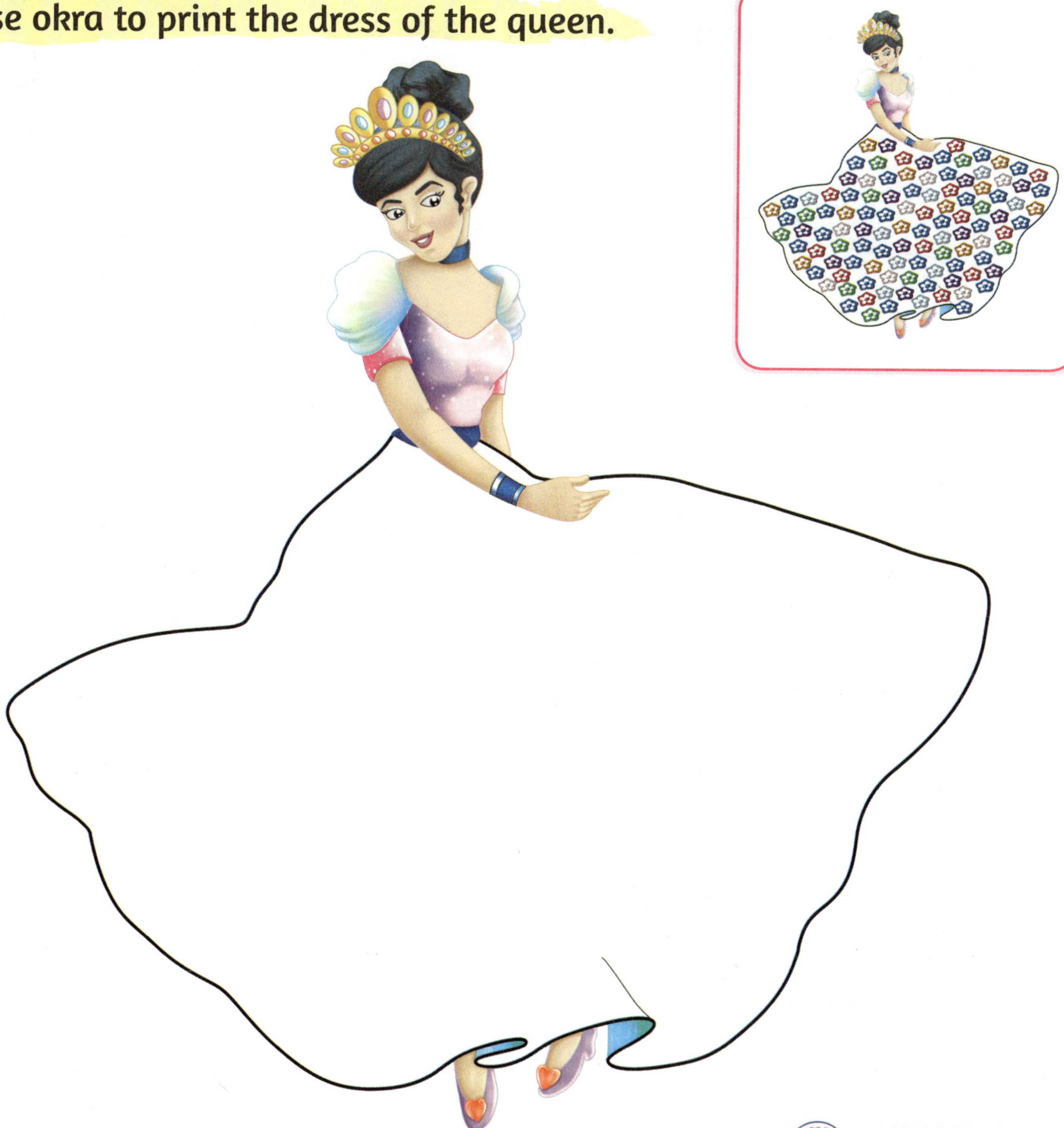

Procedure

Demonstrate how to dip the cut okra in paint and print to make the dress of the queen.

Material Required

2-3 pieces of okra and poster colours

Veggies

Create a veggie family using foam sheets and googly eyes.

Procedure

Demonstrate how to cut the foam sheets in the correct shape of the vegetables. Encourage children to do the activity independently.

Material Required

Foam sheets—yellow, brown, pink, orange, and red, child-safe scissors, glue and 5 pairs of googly eyes

Origami Kite

Make a kite using origami paper.

Step 1

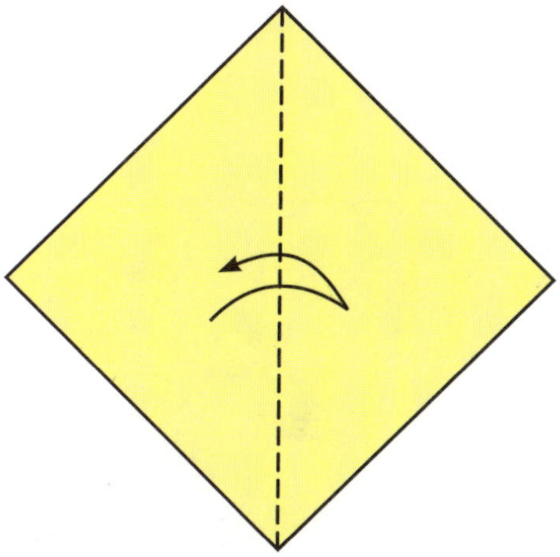

Step 2

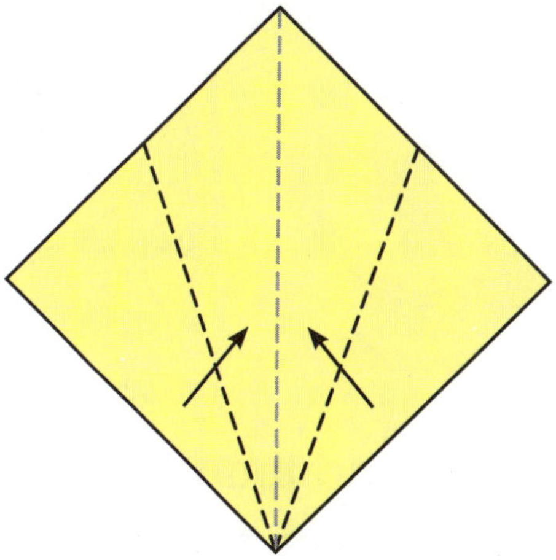

Step 3

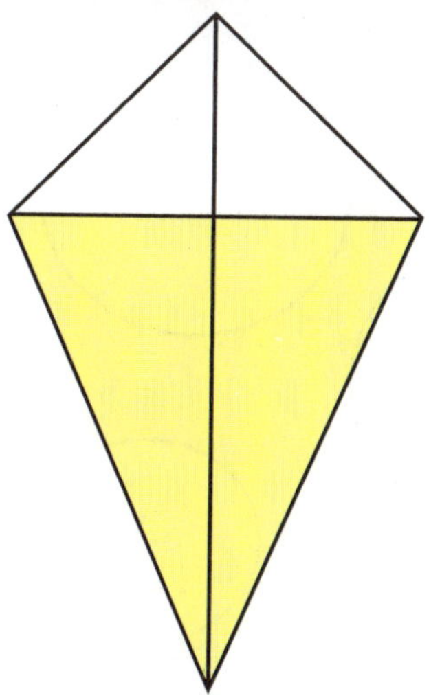

Paste here

Procedure

Follow steps to make a kite. Paste the kite and decorate it with differently coloured sketch pens.

Material Required

Origami paper, sketch pens and glue

Giraffe

Use twigs and wool to make giraffe. Paste leaves for giraffe to eat.

Material Required

Twigs, leaves, brown/orange wool and glue

Procedure

As a home assignment, children can be asked to bring twigs and leaves for this activity. They can paste these on the hollow marks of giraffe, accordingly. They should paste wool preferably orange/brown colour for the tail and hair of the giraffe. It should be made sure that children stick the pieces of wool close to each other to make giraffe's hair.

Let's Draw!

Draw and colour anything you like.

Jumbo Elephant

Let's make an elephant.

Procedure

Paste the balloon as shown in the reference image to make the face of elephant. Cut the shape of ears from the A4 sheet of paper and paste. Paste googly eyes to complete the elephant.

Material Required

A big balloon, coloured A4 paper, child-safe scissors and glue

Spray Painting

Spray paint to complete the tree.

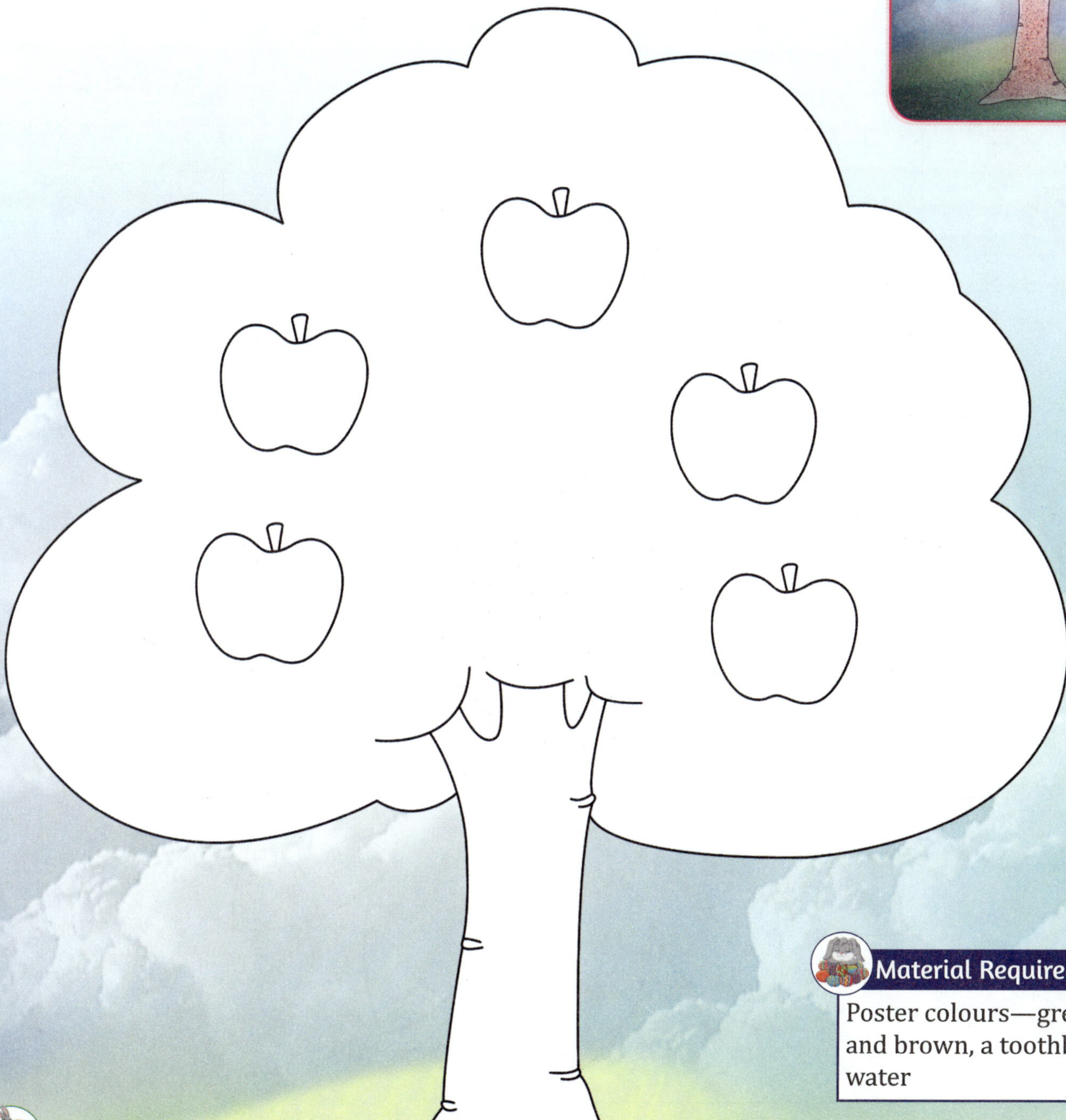

Material Required

Poster colours—green, red and brown, a toothbrush and water

Procedure

Demonstrate how to spray paint the tree using a toothbrush. To paint apples, children can smudge red paint with their index fingers and water. While doing this activity, they can cover the page with a newspaper or any rough cloth to minimize the spread of colours at unwanted places.

Spotty Sunflower

Make the sunflower. Print with cotton buds to make its seeds.

Procedure

Help children draw the sunflower in two parts such that they get two cut-outs to be pasted for the image of the sunflower. For the seeds of the sunflower, they can dip a cotton bud in black paint and print it on the seeds.

Material Required

Golden foam sheet,
black poster colour, a cotton bud,
child-safe scissors and glue

Icy Octopus

Make an octopus with pipe cleaners.

Procedure

Demonstrate how to make a big hollow capital letter 'O'. Children can cut and paste the letter on the page. With the help of pipe cleaners and tape they can make tentacles of the octopus. In the end, they can paste googly eyes to complete the octopus.

Material Required

Blue chart paper, pipe cleaners, tape and googly eyes

Straw Hut

Use ice-cream sticks and straw to make a hut.

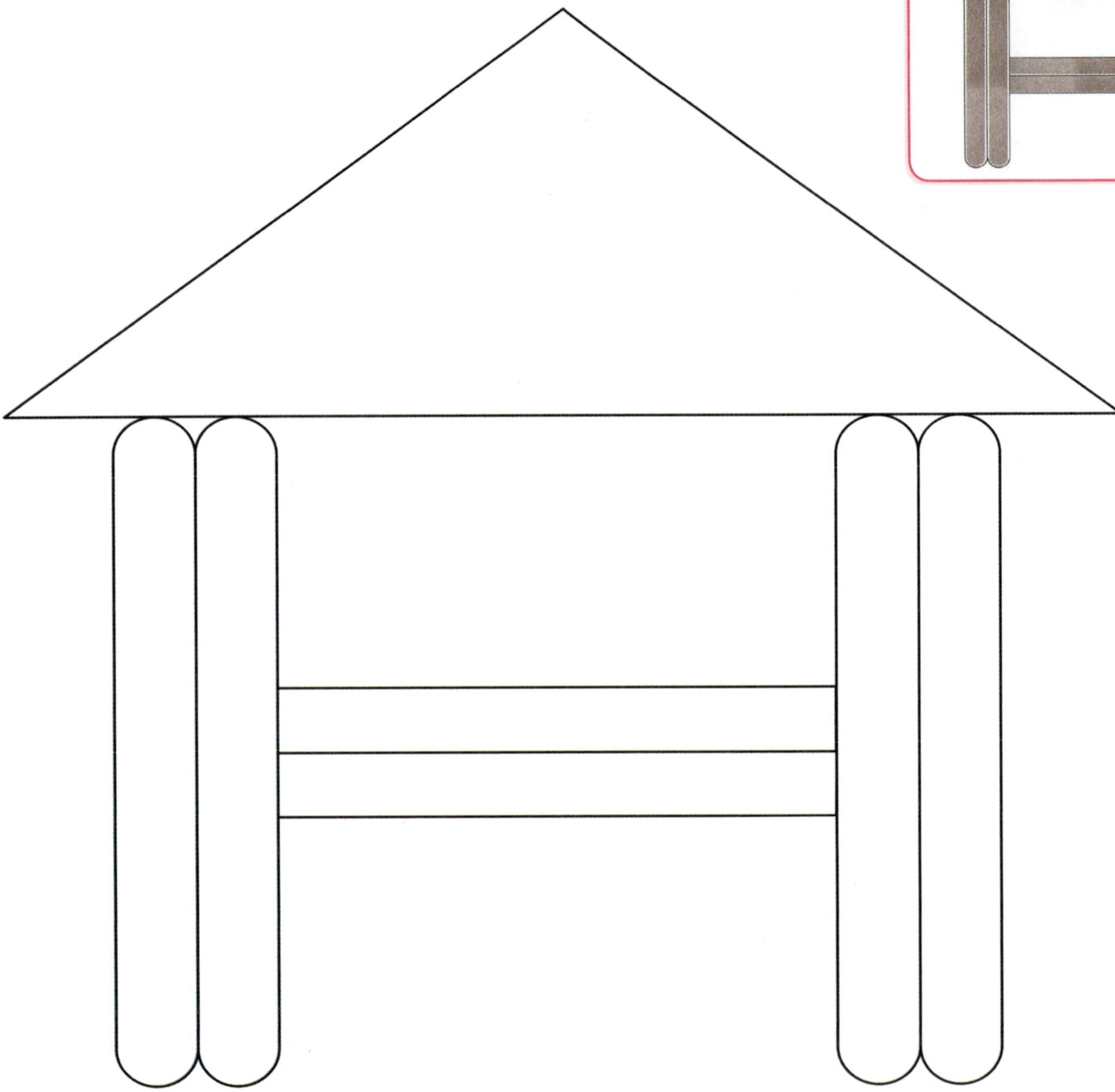

Procedure

Paint ice-cream sticks brown and paste those sticks on the hollow letter 'H' just as shown in the sample image. Paste straw over the top of the letter 'H' to complete the hut.

Material Required

Ice-cream sticks, straw, paintbrush, child-safe scissors, glue and brown poster colour

Sand Art

Complete the scenery with sand.

Material Required

Sand and glue

Procedure

First apply glue where sand has to be put. Then pour sand on those places to decorate the scenery.

Origami Cat

Make the face of a cat using origami paper.

Step 1

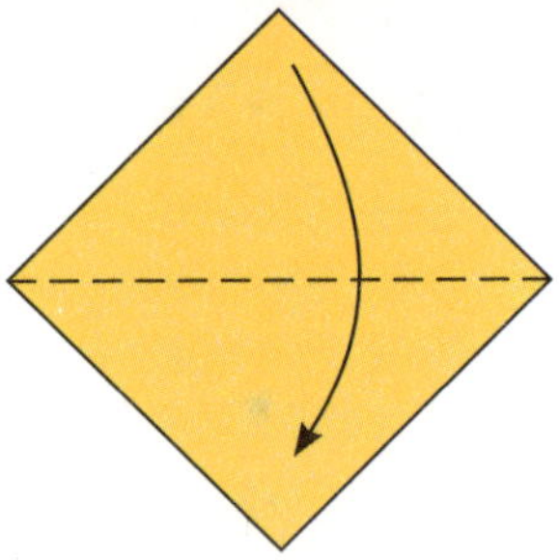

Step 2

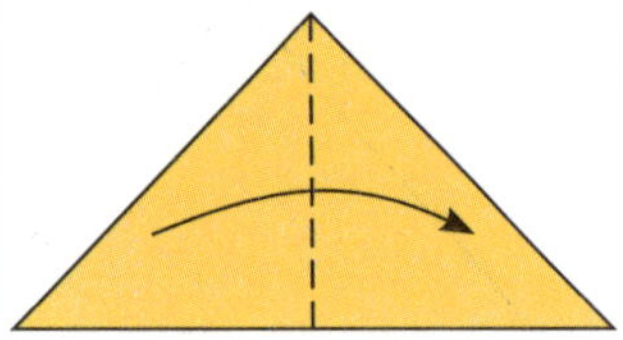

Step 3

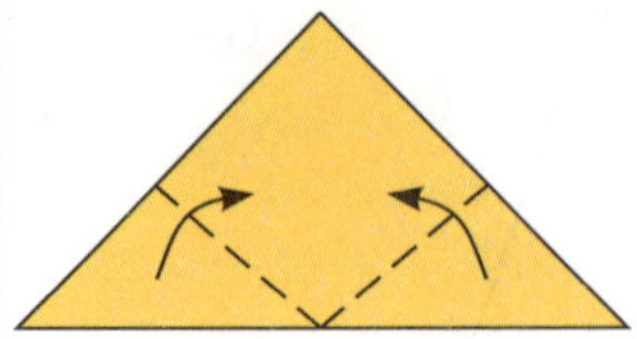

Step 4

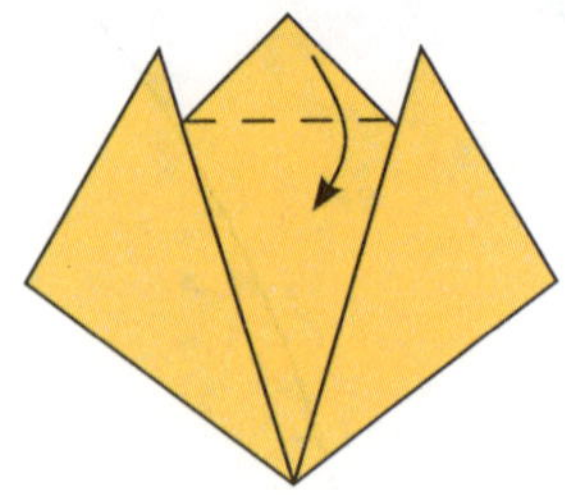

Step 5

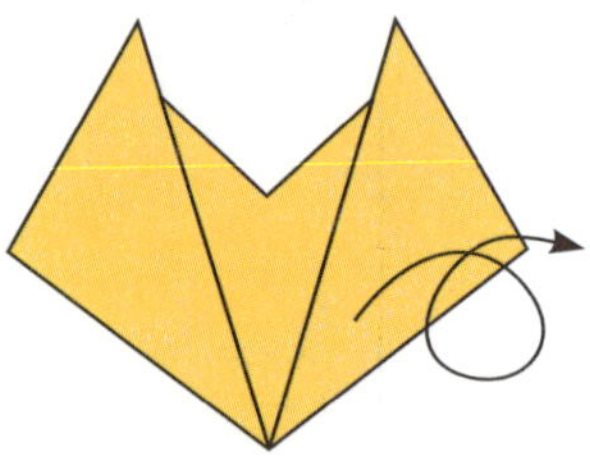

Step 6

Paste here

Procedure

Follow the steps to make the cat using origami paper. Use a black sketch pen to make the nose and the whiskers. Paste googly eyes to complete the cat.

Material Required

Origami paper, black sketch pen, googly eyes and glue

Proud Peacock

Colour and decorate the peacock.

Procedure

Using blue and green crayons, colour the head, legs, feet, and some portion of the tail of the peacock. Paste colourful beads/stickers in the same sequence/pattern as shown in the reference image.

Material Required

Colourful beads/decorative stickers, glue, blue and green crayons

Wriggly Worm

Make a worm with a sponge.

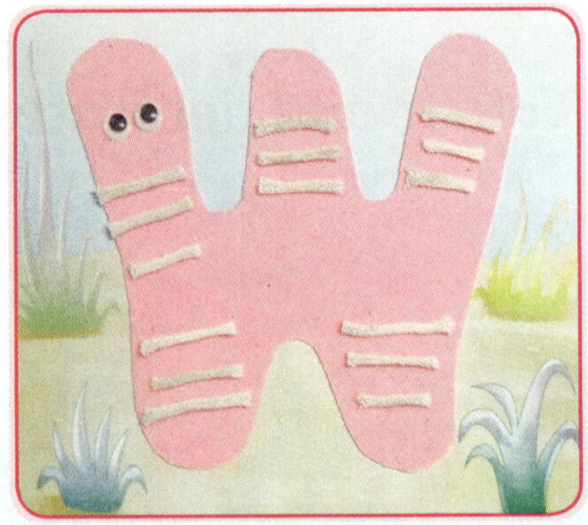

Procedure

Demonstrate how to draw and cut out capital W on a sponge. Children can cut and paste tiny pieces of wool on the worm just as in the sample picture. Either paste googly eyes for the worm or draw them using black paint.

Material Required

1 piece of coloured sponge, 2 googly eyes, wool, glue and child-safe scissors

Let's Draw!

Draw and colour anything you like.

Chirping Birds

Make birds with pista shells.

Procedure

Colour the pista shells with different poster colours. When the shells get dry, paste those on the tree to make birds. Use a black sketch pen to make their beaks, claws, eyes and tail as shown in the reference image.

Material Required

Pista shells, 2-3 poster colours, glue and black sketch pen

Draw with Numbers

Draw and colour the shark.

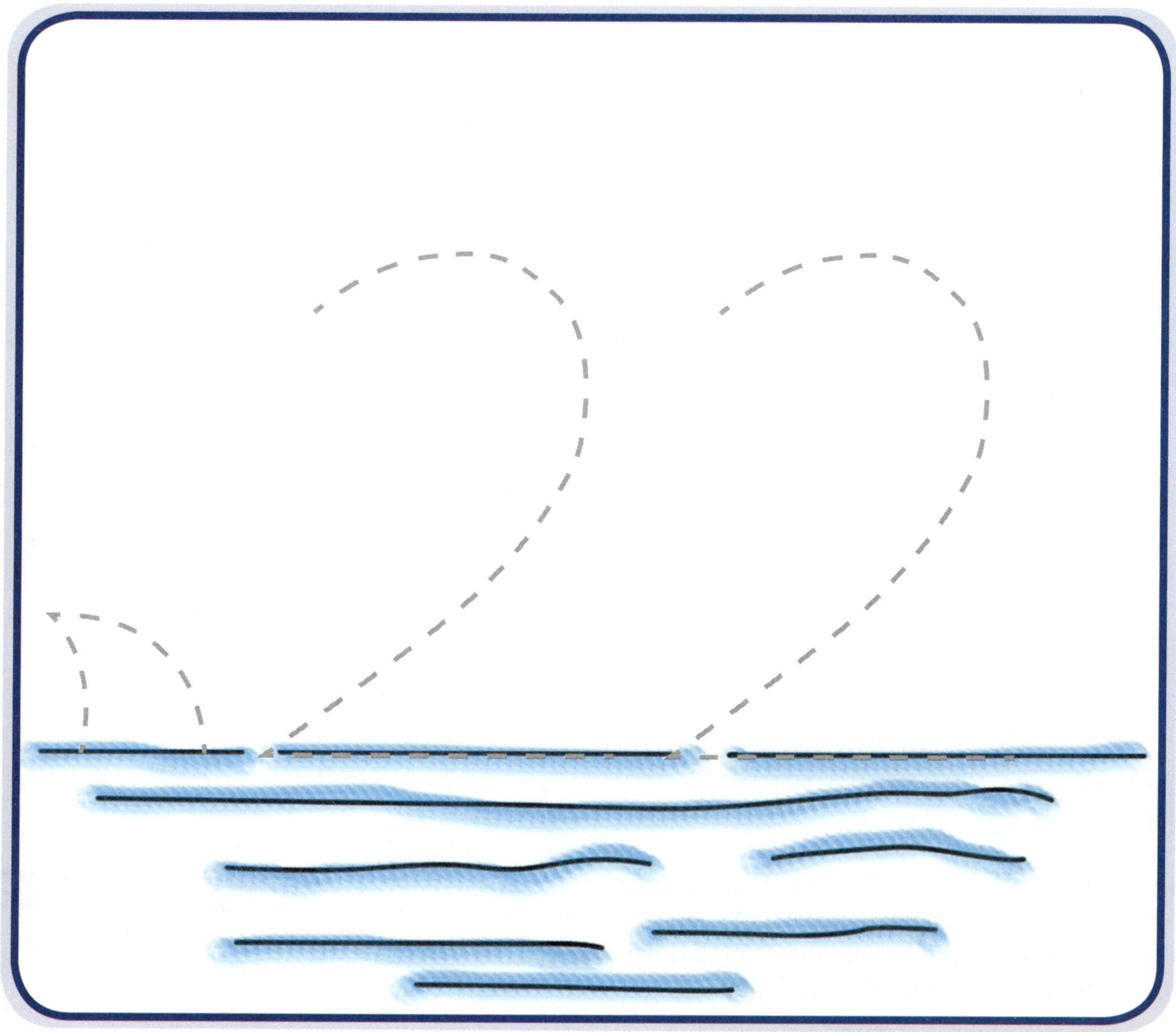

Underwater Creatures

Use felt paper to make underwater creatures.

Procedure

Demonstrate how to draw and cut out the hollow capital 'U' on the felt paper. Children can then place the letter on the centre of the page. They can again use coloured felt paper to cut shapes of circles and ovals to make fish. They can place the fish on and around the letter 'U'. They can draw the eyes of the fish using a black sketch pen.

Material Required

Sheets of felt paper, child-safe scissors, googly eyes and glue

32

Origami Cow

Make the face of a cow using origami paper.

Step 1

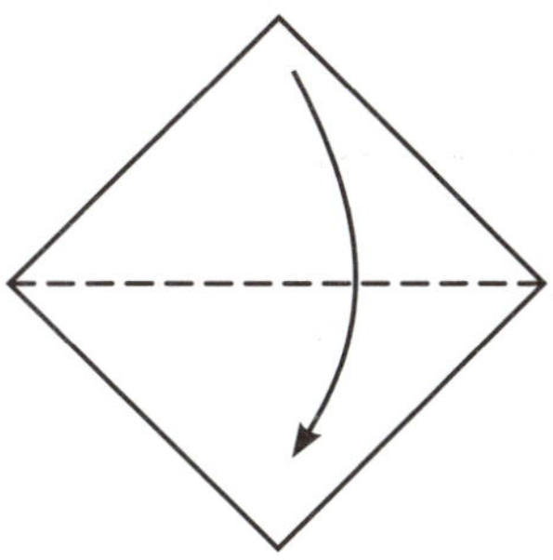

Step 2

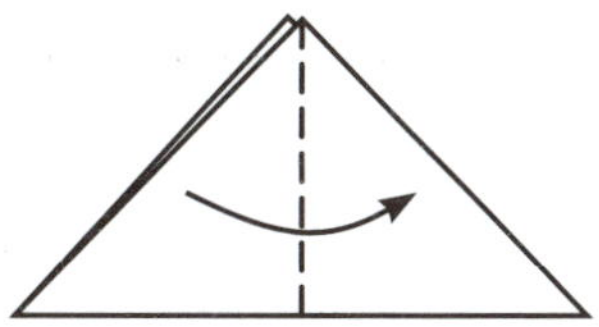

Step 3

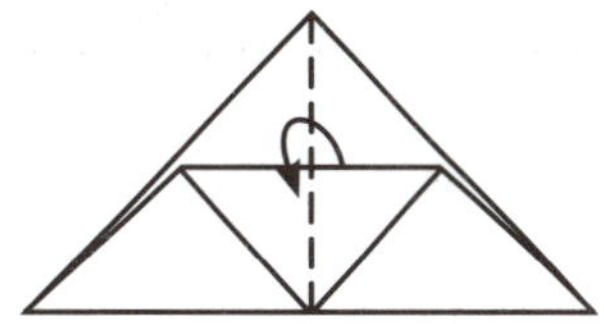

Step 4

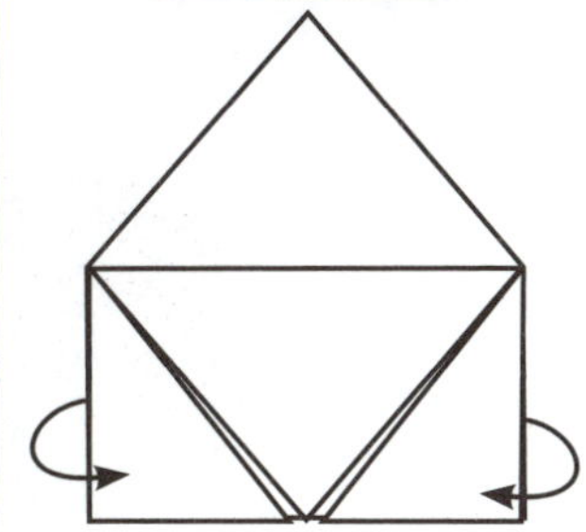

Step 5

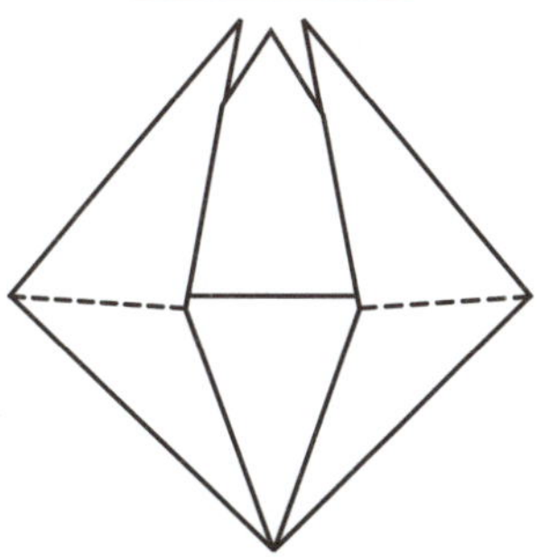

Step 6

Paste here

Procedure

Follow the steps to make the cow using white paper. Children can then cut pink origami paper to make the nose of the cow. To make horns of the cow, they can cut and paste orange origami paper on the cow (refer to the image given above). Googly eyes can be pasted and black sketch pen can be used to make spots on the cow. Once they are done with making the origami cow, they can paste it on the page.

Material Required

A4-size white paper, pink and orange origami paper, black sketch pen, child-safe scissors, googly eyes and glue

Stripy Zebra

Paste strips of black paper and lengths of black wool to make the zebra.

Procedure

Demonstrate how to cut thick but short strips of black paper and paste it on the letter. Children can then paste pieces of black wool on the zebra to make its hair. They can also use a small piece of wool to make a smile on the zebra's face.

Material Required

Black paper, child-safe scissors, black wool, black sketch pen and glue

Palm Parrot

Make colourful feathers of the parrot.

Material Required

Sheets of coloured A4 paper, child-safe scissors and glue

Procedure

Ask children to trace their hands on three differently coloured sheets. Cut out the hand print. Demonstrate how to paste them. For the first cut-out, fold it into equal halves and paste it little towards the end of the parrot's tail so that it is visible and is not overlapped by other sheets that are yet to be pasted for feathers. For the second and third cut-outs, cut those in two equal halves and paste the coloured sheets alternately to complete the colourful feathers of the parrot. Use the thumbnail to guide the pasting of the feather.

Origami Dog

Make the face of a dog using origami paper.

Step 1

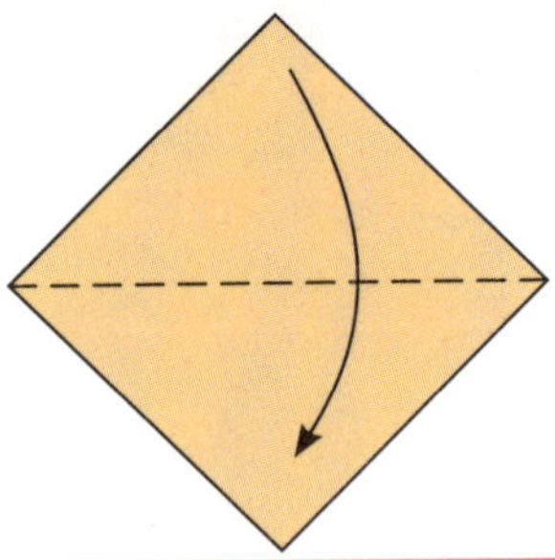

Step 2

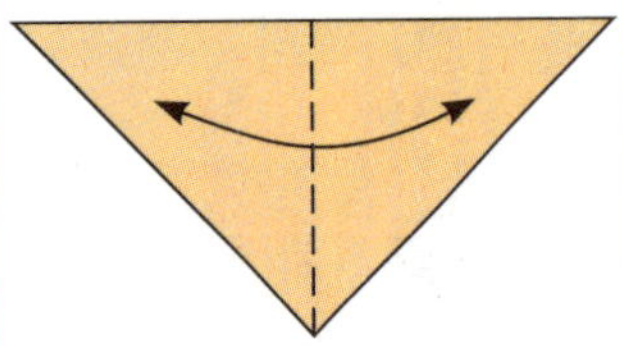

Step 3

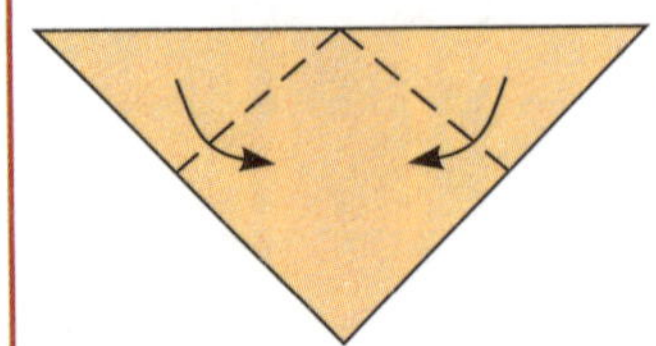

Step 4

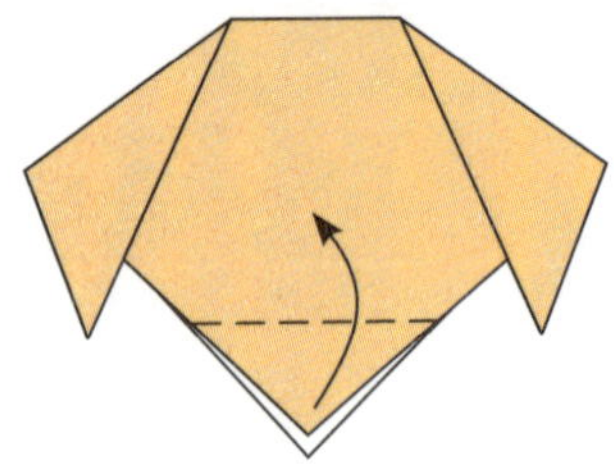

Step 5

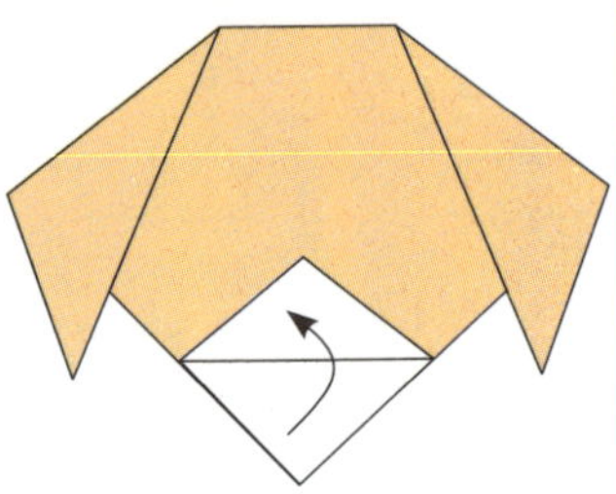

Step 6

Paste here

Procedure

Follow the steps to make the dog using origami paper. Use a black sketch pen to make the nose and the whiskers. Paste googly eyes to complete the dog.

Material Required

Origami paper, black sketch pen, googly eyes and glue

Fly By Butterfly

Make a colourful butterfly with woollen threads.

Procedure

Paste pieces of wool on the outer and inner outlines of the butterfly. Use the leftover wool to make patterns on the butterfly. At last, decorate the butterfly with glitter and beads.

Material Required

Colourful wool, glitter, tiny beads, child-safe scissors and glue

Drizzling Rain

Paste cotton on the cloud. Thumbprint 15 raindrops.

Procedure

Paste cotton within the outline of the cloud. Use a black sketch pen to outline the cloud. Dip the thumb in blue paint to print rain drops. When the paint has dried, use a black sketch pen to give black outline for each droplet. Paste googly eyes on the cloud and black paper to put a smile on it.

Material Required

Cotton, black paper sheet, black sketch pen, blue poster colour and glue

Peekaboo

Find the hidden numbers and colour them blue. Colour and complete the picture.

Wonder With Colours

Paste satin ribbons to make the rainbow.

Procedure

Paste satin ribbons in the correct sequence of colours to make a rainbow. Paste cotton to make clouds.

Material Required

7 satin ribbons—violet, indigo, blue, green, yellow, orange, red, cotton and glue

Draw with Numbers

Draw and colour the woodpecker.

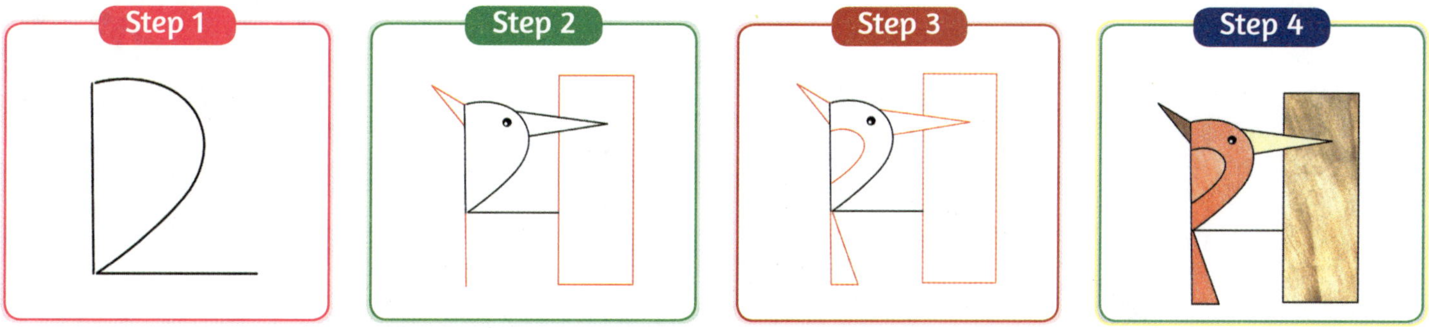

Pizza Topping

Paste beads to complete the pizza topping.

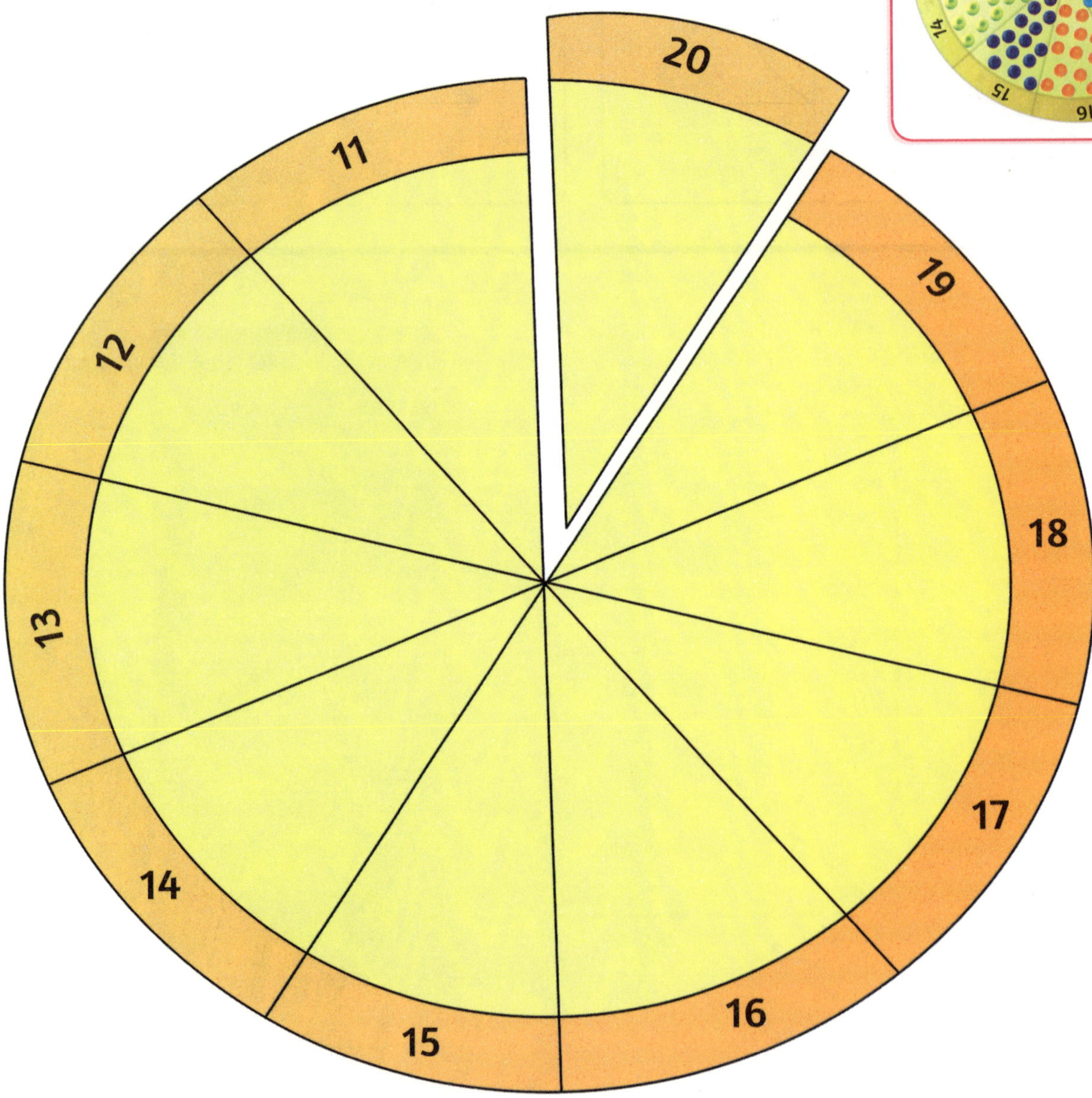

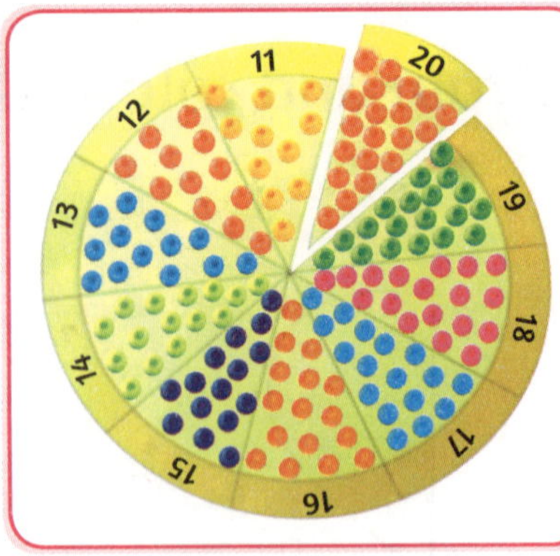

Procedure

Paste the beads on each section of the pizza. Make sure that each section of the pizza has beads of the same colour.

Material Required

Colourful beads and glue

Let's Draw!

Draw and colour anything you like.

Hello Little Fish

Use a coin to print scales on the fish.

Procedure

Take a coin and dip its edge in the paint. Now use the same edge of the coin to print the scales on the fish.

Material Required

A coin and poster colours

Draw With Numbers

Draw and colour the squirrel.

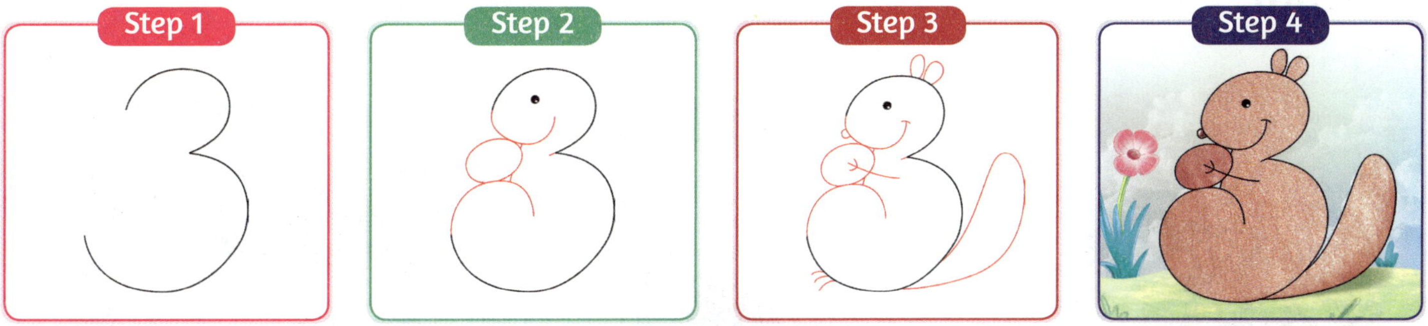

Block Printing

Take a piece of cotton cloth. Use a wooden printing block to print on the cloth.

Step 1

Step 2

Step 3

Paste here

Procedure

Dip the block in paint. Print on the cloth to make a pattern. Paste the cloth on the page.

Material Required

A piece of cotton cloth, acrylic paints, and a wooden printing block

Okra Patterns

Use okra to make a pattern as you like.

Procedure

Dip the cut okra into any colour of your choice. Print to make a design.

Material Required

2-3 okras and poster colours

Draw With Numbers

Draw and colour the whale.

Ready For Fun

Use a long piece of yarn to make a colourful thread painting.

Step 1

Step 2

Step 3

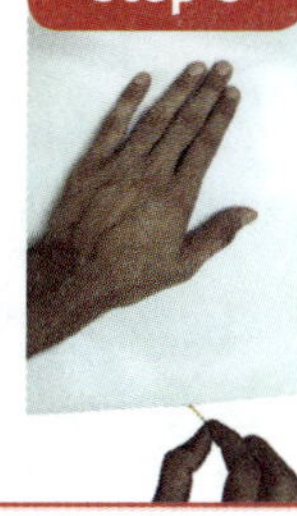

Step 4

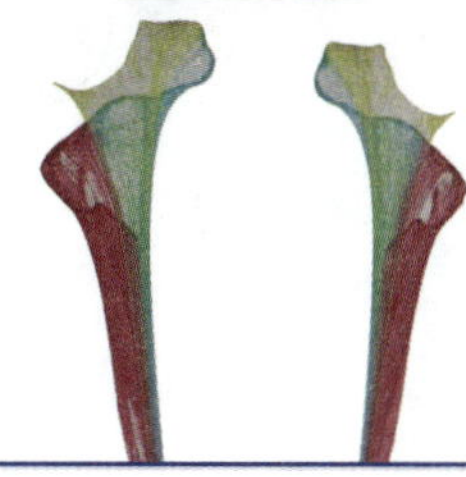

Procedure

Take a long piece of string and dip its different portions in different colours such that each portion has a single colour on it. Press the thread along its length to remove excess paint from it. Fold the white paper in half. Open the paper and place the thread on one half of the paper with an end dangling outside the paper. Fold the paper again and pull the free end of the thread sharply but gently. You will see patterns on the page.

Material Required

A piece of string, square white paper and poster colours

Let's Draw

Draw and colour anything you like.

Draw with Letters

Draw and colour the butterfly.

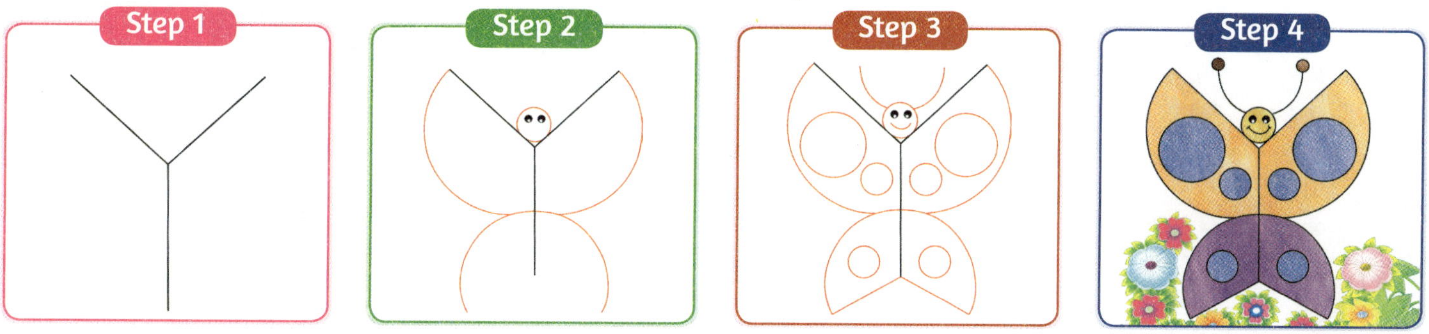

Dancing Dragonflies

Make dragonflies with rubber bands.

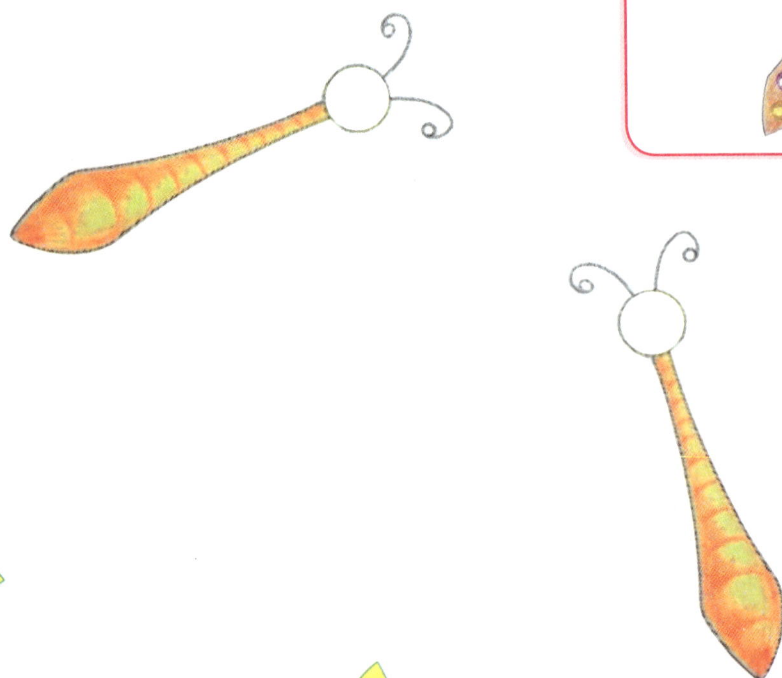

Procedure

Paste big rubber bands as shown in the picture. This will make the shape of dragonflies. Use shiny stickers to decorate tails of dragonflies. Use black sketch pen to make the eyes of dragonflies.

Material Required

Big rubber bands, glue, poster colours, shiny stickers and black sketch pen

Draw with Numbers

Draw and colour the fish.

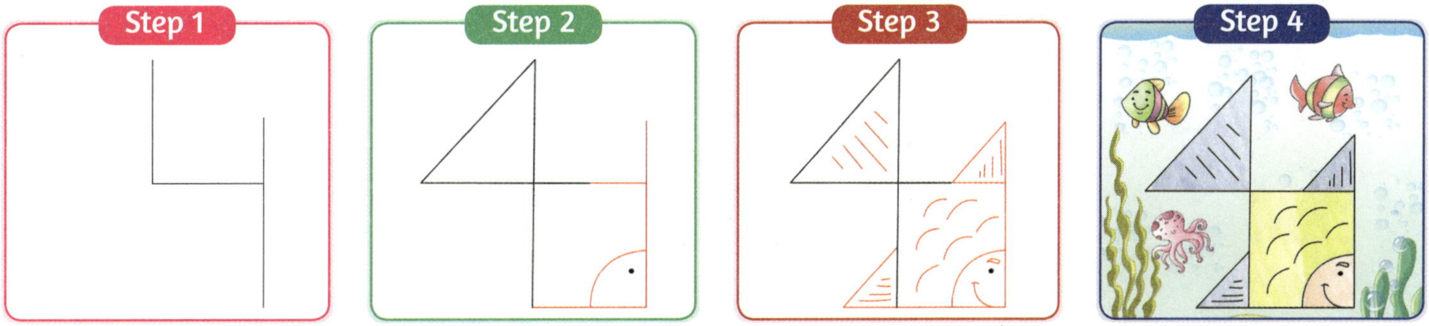

My Pretty Flowers

Paste sago to complete the flowers. Paint these yellow.

Procedure

Pick one granule of sago at a time to paste it inside the given outline. When the glue dries, use a paintbrush and yellow poster colour to paint sago.

Material Required

Sago, yellow poster colour and glue

Colour with Codes

Use the colour code and colour the picture.

Let's Draw!

Draw and colour anything you like.